WHAT'S SO AMAZING ABOUT GRACE?

UPDATED EDITION

PARTICIPANT'S GUIDE | SIX SESSIONS

PHILIP YANCEY

WRITTEN CONTRIBUTIONS BY ESTEE ZANDEE

ZONDERVAN

What's So Amazing About Grace? Participant's Guide, Updated Edition
Copyright © 2000, 2021 by Philip Yancey

Requests for information should be addressed to:
Zondervan, *3900 Sparks Dr. SE, Grand Rapids, Michigan 49546*

ISBN 978-0-310-12977-6 (softcover)

ISBN 978-0-310-12978-3 (ebook)

Cover Design: Ron Huizinga
Cover Photo: © Cavan Images | Offset.com
Interior Design: Kait Lamphere

First Printing February 2021 / Printed in the United States of America

CONTENTS

PREFACE

Little did I know what I was getting into when I began writing a book about grace. I chose the topic out of my concern that some of us in the U.S. church have lost the way of grace and that we stand in danger of becoming ineffective in our most important role to the world. As I began my research, I came to see that grace underlies the gospel. It affects how we treat each other: our family members and the coworker we don't get along with, those who sit beside us in church and those who vote in ways we don't agree with, the friend who hurt us years ago and the cranky neighbor down the street. I truly believe that the future for Christians depends on how we master the art of giving grace.

Gordon MacDonald said, "You need not be a Christian to build houses, feed the hungry, or heal the sick. There is only one thing the world cannot do. It cannot offer grace." And that is the church's single most important contribution. Where else can the world go to find grace? And the world indeed is desperately thirsty for grace.

As I look back on my own pilgrimage—marked by wanderings, detours, and dead ends—I see now that what pulled me along was my search for grace. I rejected the church for a time because I found so little grace there. I returned because I found grace nowhere else.

I have barely tasted grace myself, have rendered less than I have received, and am no "expert" on it. These are the very reasons that impelled me to write. I wanted to understand why the church seems to have lost this gift. Often the down-and-out, who flocked to Jesus, feel unwelcome among his followers. What happened? And most personally, what would it mean for us to truly understand, receive, and give the gift that God gives so generously to me and you?

I wrote the book *What's So Amazing About Grace?* at the end of the twentieth century. At the time, millions of people were rejoicing in their new freedom after the fall of communism in Europe. The United States was entering a new century with power and optimism. Since then, we have seen the rise of nationalism globally, deep political and racial divisions in the U.S., and the phenomenon of "nones" who claim no religious affiliation. The world is in desperate need of grace-dispensers.

We have produced six videos and the corresponding study sessions to help you and a study group or class to explore those very questions, learn from the example of Jesus, and reflect on what grace means for our daily lives. Most of the material in this video series is new, so those who read the book (though not necessary for group participation) will find that this participant's guide enhances their experience.

I have filled the book and this study with stories because I believe stories are the best way to comprehend grace. I hope they prompt you to reflect on and share the stories from your own experiences. Groups are an ideal place to share stories of grace and ungrace because at its core, grace is always relational.

Philip Yancey

HOW TO USE
THIS GUIDE

GROUP USE

The *What's So Amazing About Grace?* video-based curriculum is designed as an engaging experience for a small group, Bible Study, church class, or the like. To make sure everyone has time to share, it is recommended that large groups break into smaller groups of no more than six to eight people.

MATERIALS

Each member of the group should have their own participant's guide to go along with the six videos. Though not necessary, it is encouraged that each member has their own copy of the *What's So Amazing About Grace?* book for in-depth insights and an enriched experience.

FACILITATION

Groups find that studies like this one run best when a facilitator is appointed to run the video, keep discussions going, and make sure each member has a chance to share.

PERSONAL JOURNEYS

For deeper reflections, this participant's guide includes four studies per session for each member to do on their own in between group meetings. These individual studies take a closer look at biblical passages from the *What's So Amazing About Grace?* video and book and offer questions to prompt thoughts and ideas on how to apply the message of God's grace to your daily life.

CHAPTER REFERENCES AND
SUGGESTED READINGS

This participant's guide draws on the book *What's So Amazing About Grace?* [abbreviated WSAAG] by Philip Yancey. Chapter references and suggested reading notes are included throughout this guide for groups and individuals who want to read along.

NO STRINGS ATTACHED

God's Love for the Undeserving

Grace teaches us that God loves because of who God is,
not because of who we are. Categories of worthiness
simply don't apply.

—PHILIP YANCEY, *WHAT'S SO AMAZING
ABOUT GRACE?* VIDEO SESSION ONE

INTRODUCTION

In one of his last acts before his death, Jesus forgave a thief dangling on a cross, knowing full well the thief had converted out of plain fear. That thief would never study the Bible, never attend synagogue or church, and never make amends to all those he had wronged. He simply said "Jesus, remember me," and Jesus promised, "today you will be with me in paradise." It was another shocking reminder that grace does not depend on what we have done for God but rather what God has done for us. [WSAAG, chapter 4]

By instinct, we feel we must *do something* in order to be accepted, to earn our place in the world and the love and acceptance of others. This concept of earning is built into every human system—and our relationship with divine love is no exception. We work obsessively to please both other people and God. Perhaps this is why we struggle so much to comprehend God's grace, let alone embody it in our daily lives.

Many of us formed an image of a mathematical God when we became Christians: a great judge who weighs our good and evil deeds on a set of scales and somehow always finds us wanting. We miss the God of the Gospels, a God of mercy and generosity who never ceases to find ways to extend love and give us grace. [chapter 5]

WATCH VIDEO

Watch the video for session one. Add to the key points below notes of your own on anything that stands out or prompts a thought or a feeling.

Grace, like water, always flows down to the lowest level.

"Doctors like Will Cooke and C. Everett Koop looked to Jesus, the Great Physician, as their model. Jesus put it bluntly: 'It is not the healthy who need a doctor, but the sick,' he said. 'I have not come to call the righteous, but sinners.'"

Jesus healed and ministered to those deemed "undeserving" by the culture of his day: the unclean, leprosy victims, cultural outsiders and enemies like the Roman soldier, and even the bodies of the dead in order to bring them back to life.

"See to it that no one misses the grace of God" (Hebrews 12:15).

"Grace is tough, and difficult. It means showing love and compassion to people who may take advantage of it. It means forgiving those who have wounded us, and sacrificing our own interests for the sake of others."

GROUP DISCUSSION

Choose the questions that work best for your group.

1. Both Dr. Cooke and Dr. Koop faced the temptation to let judgment determine the way they served those in need. Instead, they followed the example of Jesus and let the healing power of grace determine how they treated others. Imagine putting yourself in the doctors' shoes: What part of their response would be hardest for you?

2. Jesus healed and ministered to those who were deemed the most undeserving by the culture of his day. Who are the individuals and groups considered "undeserving" of grace and second chances by our culture today? What are some examples of how you could extend grace to those individuals or groups?

3. Based on Philip's informal survey, most people don't think of the word *grace* when they think about Christians. Why do you think this is so?

4. **Read John 3:16–17.** Instead of casting divine judgment, what was Jesus's primary goal in coming to earth? What does this verse tell you about God's heart for the world?

5. By default, we can't seem to help thinking of God's grace in terms of fairness, as if we could somehow earn his free gift. How does this limit our understanding of God's true nature?

6. "Grace, like water, flows to the lowest part." What might the world look like for Christians to put this principle into action?

CLOSING PRAYER

Spend a few minutes reflecting on today's discussion, then pray the following prayer together—out loud as a group—or allow a volunteer to pray on behalf of the group. Add in your own words as you like.

> *Lord, we confess that we have practiced ways of ungrace—in our judgmental thoughts, in our reluctance to be generous and kind to others, and in the ways we have tried to earn your grace for ourselves. Please open our eyes, our hearts, and our hands that we may recognize, receive, and, in turn, pass along the gift of your grace.*

SUGGESTED READING

For more thoughts and stories about grace from Philip Yancey, read: *What's So Amazing About Grace?*, chapters 1–5.

Each reading will include stories about Philip's personal journey toward God's grace and will often highlight stories from well-known authors, movies, or historical events that illustrate the power of grace.

BETWEEN SESSIONS

These four individual studies take a closer look at biblical passages from the *What's So Amazing About Grace?* video and book and offer questions to prompt thoughts and ideas on how to apply the message of God's grace to your daily life.

PERSONAL JOURNEY 1.1

"Grace is not about finishing last or first;
it is about not counting."
—PHILIP YANCEY [WSAAG, CHAPTER 5]

Read Matthew 20:1–16.

Jesus's parable of the workers and their grossly unfair paychecks confronts the scandal of grace head-on. In a contemporary Jewish version of this story, the workers hired late in the afternoon work so hard that the employer, impressed, decides to award them a full day's wages. Not so in Jesus's version, which notes that the last crop of workers have been idly standing around in the marketplace, something only lazy, shiftless workers would do during harvest season. Moreover, these laggards do nothing to distinguish themselves, and the other workers are shocked by the pay they receive. What employer in his right mind would pay the same amount for one hour's work as for twelve!

Jesus's story makes no economic sense, and that was his intent. He was giving us a parable about grace, which cannot be calculated like a day's wages.

- Which group of workers in Jesus's parable do you relate to the most and why?

- Why does grace so often seem offensive or scandalous to us?

- Like the workers who grumbled at the generosity of the vineyard owner, when have you been envious of the gift God has given to another?

- In what ways have you been blessed by the *unfairness* of God's grace?

PRAYER

Start your prayer with these words from Isaiah and add your own words of gratitude for the ways God has given undeserved grace to you.

"'For my thoughts are not your thoughts, neither are your ways my ways,' declares the LORD. 'As the heavens are higher than the earth, so are my ways higher than your ways and my thoughts than your thoughts'" (Isaiah 55:8–9).

PERSONAL JOURNEY 1.2

"To be a Christian means to forgive the inexcusable,
because God has forgiven the inexcusable in you."
—C. S. LEWIS, *THE WEIGHT OF GLORY*

Read Matthew 18:23–35.
The parable of the unmerciful servant is an exaggeration on many levels. For the servant to owe the king such a large amount—the equivalent of several million dollars today—that his family, children, and all his property would not make a dent in repaying the debt is unrealistic to say the least. Jesus heightens the contrast by telling us that the amount the servant's colleague owed him was a mere few dollars.

Why Jesus draws the parable with such exaggerated strokes becomes clear when he reveals that the king represents God. This above all should determine our attitude toward others: a humble awareness that God has already forgiven us a debt so mountainous that beside it any person's wrongs against us shrink to the size of anthills.

• What thoughts and feelings arise in you when you read the quote by C. S. Lewis at the top of the page?

- Reflect on the ways this parable mirrors the gospel. **Read Romans 3:23–24.**

- What does the reaction of the forgiven servant tell us about human nature? Why is forgiving others so difficult for us?

- Think about the people in your life—colleagues, family, and friends. Who exemplifies grace and forgiveness? What person in your life is God prompting you to give grace or forgiveness to?

PRAYER

Start your prayer with the Lord's Prayer from Matthew 6:9–13. Ask God to reveal the depths of his forgiveness for you and the opportunities you have to extend forgiveness to others.

"Our Father in heaven, hallowed be your name, your kingdom come, your will be done, on earth as it is in heaven. Give us today our daily bread. And forgive us our debts, as we also have forgiven our debtors. And lead us not into temptation, but deliver us from the evil one." For thine is the kingdom and the power and the glory, for ever and ever, Amen.

PERSONAL JOURNEY 1.3

*"I led them with cords of human
kindness, with ties of love."*
—HOSEA 11:4

Read Hosea 3.

In an astonishing acted-out parable, God asks the prophet Hosea to marry a woman named Gomer in order to illustrate God's love for Israel. Gomer bears three children for Hosea, then abandons the family to live with another man. For a time she works as a prostitute, and it is during this period that God gives the shocking command to Hosea, "Go, show love to your wife again" (v. 1).

Gomer did not get fairness, or even justice; she got grace. Throughout the book of Hosea—especially in God's speeches which begin with sternness and dissolve into tears—it's a wonder that a God who allows himself to endure such humiliation never fails to return again and again. At the heart of the gospel is a God who deliberately surrenders to the wild, irresistible power of love.

- Rather than resting in her husband's gracious love, Gomer turned back to sources of false affection. In what ways have you done the same?

- Gomer understood she did not deserve Hosea's forgiveness and love, yet she received his gift of grace and returned home. In what areas of your life do you struggle to receive God's forgiveness?

- Humans work very hard at protecting their reputation and self-respect. Yet the act of giving grace has very little to do with either. Hosea bore the public disgrace of paying a prostitute's price to bring his wife back home, and Jesus bore the disgrace of being executed as a criminal. What would it mean for you to put grace above self-respect?

- Who in your life might you, like Hosea, extend love to again regardless of what happened in the past?

PRAYER

Start your prayer with this Psalm. Confess the ways you've withheld grace from others and ask God for the courage and opportunity to pass on his extravagant love to the people around you.

"The Lord is compassionate and gracious, slow to anger, abounding in love. . . . He does not treat us as our sins deserve or repay us according to our iniquities. For as high as the heavens are above the earth, so great is his love for those who fear him" (Psalm 103:8–11).

PERSONAL JOURNEY 1.4

*"My deepest awareness of myself is that I
am deeply loved by Jesus Christ
and I have done nothing to earn it or deserve it."*
—Brennan Manning, *The Ragamuffin Gospel*

Read Romans 8:31–39.

Philip writes, "I know how I respond to rejection letters from magazine editors and to critical letters from readers. I know how high my spirits soar when a larger than expected royalty check arrives, and how low they sink when the check is small. I know that my self-image at the end of the day depends largely on what kind of messages I have received from people. Am I liked? Am I loved? I await the answers from my friends, my neighbors, my family—like a starving man, I await the answers.

"Occasionally, all too occasionally, I sense the truth of grace. There are times when I study the parables and grasp that they are about *me*. I am the sheep the shepherd has left the flock to find, the prodigal for whom the father scans the horizon, the servant whose debt has been forgiven. I am the beloved one of God."

At a seminar, beloved author Brennan Manning said about the apostle John, "If John were to be asked, 'What is your primary identity in life?' he would not reply, 'I am a disciple, an apostle, an evangelist, an author of one of the four Gospels,' but rather, 'I am the one Jesus loves.'" [chapter 5]

- On an average day, what would you say is your primary identity?

- Imagine you came to a place where you could say your primary identity in life is as "the one Jesus loves." What would it mean for your relationships? Your work? The way you relate to God?

- What causes you to doubt your belovedness?

- When next you doubt how loved and accepted you are by God, what practical step could you take to restore your trust in your true identity?

PRAYER

Start your prayer with these words drawn from today's reading, and then add your own words of thanks for God's unconditional love.

God, I thank you for loving me so profoundly, and I trust that neither death nor life, neither my past, or my future, nor any powers or obstacles, nor anything else in all creation can separate me from your love that is in Christ Jesus, my Lord.

19

AN UNNATURAL ACT

Extending Grace When
You've Been Wronged

The gospel of grace begins and ends with forgiveness.
—PHILIP YANCEY [WSAAG, CHAPTER 7]

INTRODUCTION

Most ethicists would agree with philosopher Immanuel Kant who argued that a person should be forgiven only if he deserves it. If we left it there, we would remain, in the best case, stuck in a cycle of waiting for the other person to "earn" reconciliation or, in the worst case, a cycle of revenge. But the very word *forgive* contains the word *give*. Like grace, forgiveness has the maddening quality of being undeserved, unmerited, unfair.

God shattered the karmic law of sin and retribution by invading earth, absorbing the worst we had to offer, enduring crucifixion, and then fashioning from that cruel deed the remedy for the human condition. Calvary broke up the logjam between justice and forgiveness. By accepting onto his innocent self all the severe demands of justice, Jesus broke forever the chain of ungrace.

Forgiveness isn't easy and rarely is it completely satisfying. Nagging injustices remain, and the wounds still cause pain. We have to approach God again and again, yielding to God the residue of what we thought we had already surrendered long ago. Because the Gospels make clear the connection: God forgives our debts as we forgive our debtors. The reverse is also true: Only by living in the stream of God's grace will we find the strength to respond with grace toward others.

WATCH VIDEO

Watch the video for session two. Add to the key points below notes of your own on anything that stands out or prompts a thought or a feeling.

Grace is counterintuitive to the rules of nature.

The parables that Jesus tells center on the shocking unfairness of grace.
- The shepherd leaves the 99 to look for the one
- An employer pays the same amount to his workers regardless of how many hours they worked
- The prodigal son is welcomed home with a party

In the parable of the Prodigal Son, the grace of the father goes against fairness, justice, and society's norms. But God operates by different principles, giving grace to the undeserving.

This is what the entire Bible is about: A Father God yearning to get his family back.

GROUP DISCUSSION

Choose the questions that work best for your group.

1. Reflect on the human systems that make up our world today (cultural expectations, credit and loan programs, government policies, and the like). In what ways are they following karmic law? In what ways do they make room for grace?

2. **Read Luke 15:11–31.** In this story, what character do you most identify with?

3. In the parable of the Prodigal Son, how does the father give grace to each son?

4. Henri Nouwen saw that the core of the gospel is contained in the parable of the Prodigal Son. In what ways is this true?

5. Consider what it cost the father, and the older son, to accept the prodigal son back into the family. What is the cost—to our emotions, our lifestyle, our finances, our reputation, etc.—of giving grace to someone else?

6. Consider the father's response to the prodigal son. What kind of legacy does he hand down to his family? What kind of impact will his gift of grace have on the larger community?

CLOSING PRAYER

Spend a few minutes reflecting on today's discussion and then start your prayer with these words:

> *Lord, we are so grateful that your grace is bigger than our sense of fairness and justice. Let us always remember that you have loved us first, unconditionally and undeservedly. Now as we go about our days, please help us to show your character to the world around us by extending such grace to others.*

SUGGESTED READING

For more thoughts and stories about grace from Philip Yancey, read:

What's So Amazing About Grace?, chapters 6–7.

BETWEEN SESSIONS

These four individual studies take a closer look at biblical passages from the *What's So Amazing About Grace?* video and book and offer questions to prompt thoughts and ideas on how to apply the message of God's grace to your daily life.

PERSONAL JOURNEY 2.1

"Breaking the cycle of ungrace
means taking the initiative."
—Philip Yancey [WSAAG, chapter 7]

Read Matthew 6:12–15.
Helmut Thielicke, a German who lived through the horrors of Nazism, wrote:

This business of forgiving is by no means a simple thing.... We say, "Very well, if the other fellow is sorry and begs my pardon, I will forgive him, then I'll give in." We make of forgiveness a law of reciprocity. And this never works. For then both of us say to ourselves, "The other fellow has to make the first move." And then I watch like a hawk to see whether the other person will flash a signal to me with his eyes or whether I can detect some small hint between the lines of his letter which shows that he is sorry. I am always on the point of forgiving . . . but I never forgive. I am far too just.

Thielicke concluded that the only path beyond the law of reciprocity was in the realization that God has granted us a terrible agency: by denying forgiveness to others, we are in effect determining them unworthy of God's forgiveness, and thus so are we. In some mysterious way, divine forgiveness depends on us. Instead of waiting for his neighbor to make the first move, Thielicke must do so, defying the natural law of fairness. [WSAAG, chapter 7]

- When have you experienced a situation like what Thielicke describes? How did the situation resolve?

- Think about your closest relationships. Would someone on the outside say your relationships are mostly governed by grace or the law of reciprocity?

- Think about your relationship with God. Which best describes the way you relate to God: by grace or the law of reciprocity?

- What is one simple way you can take the initiative and extend grace in a relationship or in a situation in your life this week?

PRAYER

Start your prayer with these words from the Psalms and ask God to reveal the depths of forgiveness for you and to reveal the opportunities you have to extend forgiveness to others.

"You, Lord, are forgiving and good, abounding in love to all who call to you. Hear my prayer, Lord; listen to my cry for mercy. . . . Teach me your way, Lord" (Psalm 86:5–6, 11).

PERSONAL JOURNEY 2.2

"God loves his enemies—that is the glory of his love,
as every follower of Jesus knows."
—DIETRICH BONHOEFFER [WSAAG, CHAPTER 7]

Read Genesis 37:23–28; 45:1–7.

Genesis 37–50 has many loops and twists in the account of Joseph's reconciliation with his brothers. One moment, Joseph acted harshly and threw his brothers in jail and in the next, overcome with sorrow, he left the room to weep. He played tricks on his brothers, seized one as a hostage, accused another of stealing his silver cup. For months, maybe years, these intrigues dragged on until finally Joseph could restrain himself no longer. He summoned his brothers and dramatically forgave them.

With all its twists and turns, this story is a realistic depiction of the unnatural act of forgiveness. The brothers Joseph struggled to forgive were the very ones who had bullied him, schemed to murder him, and sold him into slavery. Because of them he had spent the best years of his youth moldering in an Egyptian dungeon. When grace finally broke through to Joseph, the sound of his grief and love echoed throughout the palace.

- Placing yourself in Joseph's shoes, how would you feel seeing your brothers for the first time years after they had sold you into slavery?

- Behind every act of forgiveness lies a wound of betrayal."
  [chapter 7] When have you felt the pain of betrayal?

- The Genesis account makes it clear that it wasn't easy
  for Joseph to forgive his brothers, which made it all the
  more powerful when he did. How do we give forgiveness
  even when we don't feel like it?

- The betrayal by his brothers set into motion a series of
  events that led to Joseph saving many lives. Consider
  the disappointments and wounds in your relationships.
  Can you think of any good that has come from those
  situations?

PRAYER

Start your prayer with these words drawn from Genesis 50:20 and continue your prayer asking God to increase your trust in him no matter what betrayals or disappointments you experience.

What humans intend for harm, you, God, intend for good to accomplish your divine will which is being done even now. Please come to my aid and help me to trust you in even the most painful situations.

PERSONAL JOURNEY 2.3

"But God's forgiveness is unconditional; it comes from a heart that does not demand anything for itself, a heart that is completely empty of self-seeking."
—HENRI NOUWEN [WSAAG, CHAPTER 7]

Read Jonah 3:10–4:4.

Henri Nouwen wrote,

It is this divine forgiveness that I have to practice in my daily life. It calls me to keep stepping over all my arguments that say forgiveness is unwise, unhealthy and impractical. It challenges me to step over all my needs for gratitude and compliments. Finally, it demands of me that I step over that wounded part of my heart that feels hurt and wronged and that wants to stay in control and put a few conditions between me and the one whom I am asked to forgive.

Though wrong does not disappear when we forgive, it loses its grip on us and is taken over by God, who knows what to do. Such a decision involves risk, of course: the risk that God may not deal with the person as we would want—like the prophet Jonah who resented God for being more merciful than the Ninevites deserved. [WSAAG, chapter 7]

- Jonah had decent reasons for his reluctance to give grace to the Ninevites, who were members of the oppressive and cruel Assyrian empire. What reasons have you had in withholding grace, forgiveness, or acceptance from others?

- We often grapple to control our world as much as possible. How do grace and control relate? How do they compare?

- Romans 12:19 says, "Do not take revenge, my dear friends, but leave room for God's wrath, for it is written: 'It is mine to avenge; I will repay, says the Lord.'" What does this verse mean for the way we should forgive others?

- What is the fear beneath our reluctance to completely trust God to do justice, to make things right again?

PRAYER

Start your prayer with these words from the Psalms. Continue praying that God will ready your heart to forgive freely as God forgives.

"Blessed is the one whose transgressions are forgiven, whose sins are covered. Blessed is the one whose sin the LORD does not count against them and in whose spirit is no deceit" (Psalm 32:1–2).

PERSONAL JOURNEY 2.4

"Only the experience of being forgiven makes it possible for us to forgive."

Read Romans 12:19–21 and Psalm 62:6–7.

Philip writes about a time when he read Romans 12 and was struck by verse 19. "Do not take revenge, my dear friends, but leave room for God's wrath, for it is written: 'It is mine to avenge; I will repay,' says the Lord."

"At last I understood: in the final analysis, forgiveness is an act of *faith*. In withholding forgiveness, we, in effect, are saying that we do not trust God to work out justice. We are saying that we know better than he does. By contrast, when we forgive another, we are trusting that God is the divine justice-maker. Through the act of forgiving, we release our own rights to get even and leave all issues of fairness for God to work out. We leave in God's hands the scales that must balance justice and mercy." [WSAAG, chapter 7]

The Gospels are clear about why Jesus commanded us to love our enemies, ". . . that you may be children of your

Father in heaven. He causes his sun to rise on the evil and the good, and sends rain on the righteous and the unrighteous" (Matthew 5:45).

We can trust God, our refuge and fortress, to make things right.

- How is grace related to trust? How is resentment and ungrace related to trust?

- What ways do we seek revenge and try to exact justice in our relationships and in our daily lives?

- When you make a mistake or fail in some way, do you trust God to put things to right again or do you punish yourself?

- How can we practice faith when we feel the frustration of injustice?

PRAYER

Start your prayer with these words from the Psalms. Continue praying that God will strengthen your faith and increase your trust in him.

"Praise the LORD, my soul, and forget not all his benefits— who forgives all your sins and heals all your diseases, who redeems your life from the pit and crowns you with love and compassion, who satisfies your desires with good things so that your youth is renewed like the eagle's. The LORD works righteousness and justice for all the oppressed" (Psalm 103:2–6).

THE ART OF FORGIVING

Responding with Grace When It Seems Impossible

When you forgive someone, you slice away the wrong from the person who did it. You disengage that person from his hurtful act. You recreate him.

—LEWIS SMEDES [WSAAG, CHAPTER 8]

INTRODUCTION

The gracious miracle of God's forgiveness was made all the more possible and profound because of the linkage that occurred when God came to earth in Christ. Somehow God had to come to terms with these creatures he desperately wanted to love—but how? We humans need to trust that God understands what it's like to be tempted to sin, to have a trying day, to *feel* the impossibility of forgiving another. Coming to earth and assuming a human body, a human life, God put himself on our side.

Jesus bridged the gap; he took our side all the way. And because he did, Jesus can present our case to the Father. He has been there. He understands.

From the Gospel accounts, it seems forgiveness was not easy for God either. "If it is possible, may this cup be taken from me," Jesus prayed, contemplating the cost as sweat rolled off him like drops of blood. There was no other way. Finally, in one of his last statements before dying, he did the inhumanly, impossible thing. He said, "Forgive them"—meaning all of those who had not repented: the Roman soldiers, the religious leaders, his disciples who had fled in darkness, you, me—"Forgive them, for they do not know what they are doing."

WATCH VIDEO

Watch the video for session three. Add to the key points below notes of your own on anything that stands out or prompts a thought or a feeling.

We are called to love our enemies and pray for those who persecute us.

The more we love our enemies, the more we resemble God the Father.

Jesus forgave us in advance, in order to set us free to forgive those who wrong us.

Forgiveness is humanly impossible in some situations, but because of Jesus it is possible in even the worst situations.

GROUP DISCUSSION

Choose the questions that work best for your group.

1. Philip tells three stories of radical forgiveness: Chris Carrier who forgave the man who kidnapped and attempted to kill him; Australian missionary Gladys Staines who forgave the people who burned her husband and sons alive; and Anthony Thompson who forgave the shooter at Emanuel Church. Which story is most powerful to you and why?

2. Through Jesus, God intimately understands our experiences. What does this mean for the way we relate to God? What does this mean for the way we extend forgiveness or unforgiveness to others?

3. Is forgiveness ever inappropriate, immoral, or impossible?

4. Does God ever refuse to forgive?

5. **Read Matthew 5:43–48.** Philip said, "The more we love our enemies, the more we resemble God the Father." What does this mean for the way we should seek to go about our daily lives, our relationships, our work?

6. What must we do to receive God's supernatural help in forgiving others?

CLOSING PRAYER

Spend a few minutes reflecting on today's discussion and then start your prayer with these words:

> *Lord, we are grateful that you are kind and gracious to the righteous and the wicked, to the good and those who struggle to do good, because we know we are both. Thank you for forgiving us at Calvary, even before we repented. Give us willing hearts and help us to follow your example to love our enemies, forgive others before they ask, and let your grace guide our every choice.*

SUGGESTED READING

For more thoughts and stories about grace from Philip Yancey, read:

What's So Amazing About Grace?, chapters 8–9.

BETWEEN SESSIONS

These four individual studies take a closer look at biblical passages from the *What's So Amazing About Grace?* video and book and offer questions to prompt thoughts and ideas on how to apply the message of God's grace to your daily life.

PERSONAL JOURNEY 3.1

"Justice has a good and righteous and rational kind of power. The power of grace is different: unworldly, transforming, supernatural."
—PHILIP YANCEY [WSAAG, CHAPTER 8]

Read Luke 23:33–43.

There is a terrible crystalline logic to unforgiveness. Unforgiveness always seems more rational, more justified than forgiveness. To not repay an insult would betray our honor, to not strike against the enemy would betray ancestors and the sacrifices they made. There is one major flaw in this logic, however: it never perfectly settles the score.

Kangaroo courts of Judea found a way to inflict a sentence

of capital punishment on the only perfect man who ever lived. Roman soldiers, Pilate, Herod, and members of the Sanhedrin were "just doing their jobs"—the excuse later used to explain Auschwitz, My Lai, and the Gulag—but Jesus stripped away that institutional veneer and spoke to the human heart. It was forgiveness they needed, more than anything else. Jesus had more than his executioners in mind when he spoke those final words, "Father, forgive them . . ." He had us in mind. From the cross, Jesus pronounced his own terms of repayment, striking an eternal blow against the law of unforgiveness.

- What reasons have you had for waiting to give, or refusing to give, forgiveness to another? What reasons have others had for holding a grudge against you?

- Where have you seen the chain of unforgiveness play out where individuals or groups are caught in a cycle of evening the score? What is the end result?

- **Read 1 Corinthians 2:14–16.** What does this verse tell us about the difference between human thought and the mind of Christ?

- Our Western culture prioritizes rational thought over emotional or spiritual wisdom. What does this tell us about the way we give, receive, and talk about forgiveness?

PRAYER

Start your prayer with the following words drawn from Romans 12:1–2. Continue praying that God will transform your mind to better align with his ways of grace.

Lord Christ, in your mercy, please transform my thoughts and reason by renewing my mind so that I can recognize and put into practice your good, pleasing, and perfect will.

51

PERSONAL JOURNEY 3.2

"Magnanimous forgiveness allows the possibility
of transformation in the guilty party."
—PHILIP YANCEY [WSAAG, CHAPTER 8]

Read John 21:15–17.

Forgiveness has two great powers: it can halt the cycle of blame and pain, breaking the pattern of ungrace; and it can loosen the stranglehold of guilt in the perpetrator.

Forgiveness—undeserved, unearned—can cut the cords and let the oppressive burden of guilt roll away. The resurrected Jesus led Peter by the hand through a threefold liturgy of forgiveness. Where Peter denied Jesus three times, Jesus prompts Peter to state his love for him three times—thus redeeming the harm done. Peter need not go through life with the guilty, hangdog look of one who has betrayed the Son of God. Oh, no. On the back of such transformed sinners Christ would build his church.

- When was the last time you were forgiven by someone else? What emotions did you feel in receiving grace? How did your behavior change?

- When was the last time you gave forgiveness to another person? What emotions did you feel in giving grace? How did your behavior change?

- Reflect on your relationship with God. Do you generally feel guilt, or grace?

- As Christians, we have firsthand experience receiving God's undeserved grace. Why then is giving grace still so difficult?

PRAYER

Start your prayer with the following words adapted from Romans 8:1–4. Continue praying that God will reveal the opportunities you have to better receive and live in his grace and freedom.

Lord, thank you for your gift of forgiveness and salvation, and the gracious freedom that I can live in today as a result. I know there is no condemnation for me in Christ Jesus, who gives life and freedom from sin. Now, through your Spirit, help me to truly live in that grace and freedom in word, thought, and deed.

PERSONAL JOURNEY 3.3

"Forgiveness has its own extraordinary power which reaches beyond law and beyond justice."
—PHILIP YANCEY [WSAAG, CHAPTER 8]

Read Leviticus 6:4–5.

It's commonly thought that forgiveness, prematurely given, short-circuits justice. Philip's friend works in the inner city and sees the results of evil from child abuse, drugs, and violence. "If I know something is wrong and 'forgive' without addressing the wrong, what am I doing?' he asks. 'I am potentially enabling rather than freeing." Some wrongs require restitution.

Lewis Smedes suggests forgiving those who wronged you while still insisting on a just punishment for that wrong. Forgiveness—and only forgiveness—can begin to thaw the heart of the guilty party. [WSAAG, chapter 8]

- What is the difference between giving grace and enabling?

- As Christians—forgiven by a just and gracious God—is it right for us to demand restitution for ourselves? What about for others?

- "Forget and forgive" is a common piece of advice. Is it always wise, or even possible?

- Micah 6:8 says, "He has shown you, O mortal, what is good. And what does the LORD require of you? To act justly and to love mercy and to walk humbly with your God." What does this verse tell us about how we are to live?

PRAYER

Start your prayer with the following words from the prophet Isaiah. Continue praying that God will teach you how to live according to his justice and mercy.

> *"The LORD longs to be gracious to you; therefore he will rise up to show you compassion. For the LORD is a God of justice. Blessed are all who wait for him!" (Isaiah 30:18).*

PERSONAL JOURNEY 3.4

*"When moments of grace do occur, the world
must pause, fall silent, and acknowledge that
indeed forgiveness offers a kind of cure."*
—PHILIP YANCEY [WSAAG, CHAPTER 9]

Read Acts 9:1–18.

Saul had been persecuting the fledgling Church for some time. His zealous work made it a nightmare for Christians in Jerusalem, and he also hunted down those who fled the city. He even participated in public stonings, such as that of Stephen (Acts 7). So it was a profound act that God confronted Saul on the road to Damascus and granted him a second chance. And it was no small act for Ananias to reveal his identity as a Christian to Saul. Ananias played a key role as God's messenger of grace and healing, inviting the former persecutor into the fellowship of believers. His risky, radical, undeserved acts resulted in Saul becoming the apostle Paul, who led the young church into maturity and was known as one of the greatest evangelists in history.

As Elizabeth O'Connor said, "To bless the people who have oppressed our spirits, emotionally deprived us, or in other ways handicapped us, is the most extraordinary work any of us will ever do."

- Do you think Saul should have somehow paid for the harm he caused? Why?

- What role did the supernatural help play in Saul's forgiveness?

- What lessons about Ananias's relationship with God and his actions can we learn?

- Where do you see yourself in Saul's story? Where do you see yourself in Ananias's?

PRAYER

Start your prayer with these words from the Psalms. Continue praying and ask God to grant you help to following the commands to forgive and be gracious toward others.

"I have sought your face with all my heart; be gracious to me according to your promise. I have considered my ways and have turned my steps to your statutes. I will hasten and not delay to obey your commands" (Psalm 119:58–60).

GRACE PUT TO THE TEST

Grace in the Face of Disagreement

No matter how it looks at any given point in history, the gates guarding the powers of evil will not withstand an assault by grace.

—Philip Yancey [WSAAG, Chapter 10]

INTRODUCTION

Martin Luther King, Jr. developed a sophisticated strategy of war fought with grace, not gun powder. He never refused to meet with his adversaries. He opposed policies, not personalities. Most importantly, he countered violence with nonviolence and hatred with love. "The end is reconciliation," King said. "The end is redemption; the end is the creation of the beloved community."

Philip writes, "Today as I look back on my racist childhood I feel shame, remorse, and also repentance. It took years for God to break through my armor of blatant racism—I wonder if any of us sheds its more subtle forms—and I now see that sin as one of the most malevolent, with perhaps the greatest societal impact."

Because it goes against human nature, forgiveness must be taught and practiced, as one would practice any difficult craft. "Forgiveness is not just an occasional act: it is a permanent attitude," said Martin Luther King, Jr. What greater gift could Christians give to the world than the forming of a culture that upholds, instead of hatred and racism, grace and forgiveness. [chapter 10]

WATCH VIDEO

Watch the video for session four. Add to the key points below notes of your own on anything that stands out or prompts a thought or a feeling.

We are living in a very divided time, which makes grace all the more difficult to give yet all the more powerful.

Churches are among the groups most resistant to change.

Rather than in the public sphere, true reconciliation is more likely to take place in quieter, smaller groups, person to person.

As seen in the examples of Steve Miller and Bryan Stevenson, justice must start with truth, acknowledging the sins of our past, and then work toward reconciliation.

God does not show favoritism. Jesus's death broke down the walls of division between people.

GROUP DISCUSSION

1. In what ways have you experienced racism, prejudice, and division in your community? In your family?

2. Where does division come from?

3. Churches are among those who are most resistant to change. Why is this?

4. What needs to happen for churches to become places of true reconciliation?

5. What would it look like for you to bring grace into those situations of division and ungrace?

6. **Read Galatians 3:26–29 and Genesis 1:26–27.** What do these passages tell us about God's heart for all people? What do they mean for the way we treat other people?

CLOSING PRAYER

Spend a few minutes reflecting on today's discussion and then start your prayer with these words.

Gracious God, we so easily default to our human tendencies to withhold grace, to perpetuate harm in our twisted sense of justice, and to treat others as inferior to ourselves. We humbly admit the ways we have hurt our brothers and sisters—on purpose and by accident—and thereby dishonored the divine image they carry. Soften our hearts and teach us to see all people the way you do, to love as you love, and to forgive as you forgive.

SUGGESTED READING

For more thoughts and stories about grace from Philip Yancey, read:

What's So Amazing About Grace?, chapters 10–12.

BETWEEN SESSIONS

These four individual studies take a closer look at biblical passages from the *What's So Amazing About Grace?* video and book and offer questions to prompt thoughts and ideas on how to apply the message of God's grace to your daily life.

PERSONAL JOURNEY 4.1

*"All the nations you have made will come
and worship before you, Lord; they will bring
glory to your name. For you are great and
do marvelous deeds; you alone are God."*

—Psalm 86:9–10

Read Acts 10:19–33.

The Levitical law that Israelites like Peter followed made a precise distinction between clean and unclean foods, clean and unclean animals, and clean and unclean people. No worshiper could bring a maimed or defective lamb to the temple, for God deserved the best. Gentile nonbelievers could visit the temple, but they had to stay in a sectioned-off area called the Court of the Gentiles.

Then, three times in a vision, God told Peter, "Do not call anything impure that God has made clean." This one sentence would have been scandalous to Peter. Its implications shifted his entire lifestyle—from the food he ate to whose house he could enter. After losing the argument with God on the rooftop, Peter made the concession to break Jewish law and enter the house of the Roman centurion to share the gospel. A revolution of grace was under way, one that Peter could hardly comprehend.

- Peter's reluctance to change his diet or visit the centurion wasn't so much an act of ungrace as it was an attempt to obey the laws God had given the Israelites generations before. How should we balance obedience and grace?

- What does Peter's vision tell us about who gets access to God and who doesn't? See Acts 10:34–35.

- What does Peter's vision tell us about how we should view people who are different from us?

- What individual or group is the hardest for you to extend grace to, and why?

PRAYER

Start your prayer with these words drawn from Isaiah 43:18–19. Continue praying and ask God to open your eyes to the new, perhaps surprising, ways he is moving in your life now.

Holy Father, help me to be willing to let go of old ways, to not fixate on the past when you prompt me to move in new ways. You are always making paths where before there was no way. And because of that, I now have direct access to your presence. Thank you.

PERSONAL JOURNEY 4.2

*"God may be the Sovereign Lord of the Universe,
but through his Son, God has made himself as
approachable as any doting human father."*
—PHILIP YANCEY [WSAAG, CHAPTER 12]

Read Matthew 27:46–53.

The temple in Jerusalem was organized into different areas. Gentiles worshiped in the farthest place from the altar, excluded from the main sanctuary. Jewish women could enter the main floor, but only in the women's zone. Jewish laymen had a spacious area near the front, yet even they could not approach the platform, reserved for priests alone.

The back of the platform, where the altar stood, was called the Most Holy Place, where the presence of God dwelt. And setting this area off from the rest of the temple was a foot-thick curtain. No one went behind the curtain except one priest and only once a year on the holy day of Yom Kippur. The very architecture reminded Israelites that God was set apart, other, *holy.* But the day Jesus gave his life for us, the curtain ripped open, top to bottom, in a stunning sign of the intimate, direct access *all* people now have to the holy God.

- Reflect on your relationship with God. Do you generally relate to God as one who worships and prays from afar or as one who has intimate, direct access to God's attentive presence?

- Sometimes we put up a sort of curtain in our hearts, walling off an unwanted trait or emotion, or an uncomfortable moment in our past from God out of the fear of being rejected. In what way have you done this in your life?

- What would it mean for you to bring all of yourself, the good and the bad, into the sphere of God's grace?

- Many people feel closed off from God, the church, and Christians out of fear or anger at the ways we might judge them. What are some simple, practical things you can do to invite others into the presence of God?

PRAYER

Say these words from Hebrews as a prayer and continue speaking to God, giving thanks for making a way for you into his holy and gracious presence.

"Since we have confidence to enter the Most Holy Place by the blood of Jesus, by a new and living way opened for us through the curtain, that is, his body, and since we have a great priest over the house of God, let us draw near to God with a sincere heart" (Hebrew 10:19–22).

PERSONAL JOURNEY 4.3

"As you go, proclaim this message: 'The kingdom of heaven has come near.' Heal the sick, raise the dead, cleanse those who have leprosy, drive out demons. Freely you have received; freely give."
—MATTHEW 10:7–8

Read Luke 8:42b–48.

The Levitical laws guarded against contagion: contact with a sick person, a Gentile, a corpse, certain animals, even mildew and mold could contaminate a person. But Jesus reversed the process. He constantly exposed himself to unclean people—the demon-possessed madman, the newly deceased daughter of a synagogue ruler, and a woman with a twelve-year hemorrhage. But instead of being contaminated, he made the other person whole. The naked madman did not pollute Jesus; he was freed. The dead girl did not contaminate Jesus; she was resurrected.

And the desperate woman with the flow of blood did not shame Jesus and make him unclean; she went away healed.

We ourselves can be agents of God's holiness, for God now dwells within us. In the midst of an unclean world we can stride, as Jesus did, seeking ways to be a source of holiness. We are called upon to be conveyors of grace, not avoiders of contagion.

- What are the contagious, unclean sources in your community and culture today?

- First John 4 tells us that the One who is in us is greater than he who is in the world. How can we make sure that our confidence in God's desire to heal and love the world overrides our fear of being "contaminated?"

- In Luke 8, Jesus healed the bleeding woman even before he had heard her story. What does this tell us about the way we should treat people who we think are immoral or unclean?

- Think about your life at home with your family, at work, at church, and in your community. What would it look like for you to be an agent of holiness in those circles?

PRAYER

Start your prayer with this verse from the Psalms and continue praying that God will equip you to be an agent of holiness to your world.

*"The LORD is my light and my salvation—whom shall I fear?
The LORD is the stronghold of my life—of whom shall I be afraid?" (Psalm 27:1).*

PERSONAL JOURNEY 4.4

"We're all oddballs, but God loves us anyway."
—PHILIP YANCEY [WSAAG, CHAPTER 12]

Read Matthew 21:12–16.

The Gospels record only one occasion when Jesus resorted to violence: the cleansing of the temple. Brandishing a makeshift whip, he overturned tables and benches and drove out the merchants who had set up shop there. The very architecture of the temple expressed the Jewish hierarchy: Gentiles could enter only the outer court. Jesus resented that merchants had turned the Gentiles' area into a bazaar filled with the sounds of animals bleating and merchants haggling over prices, an atmosphere hardly conducive to worship.

Immediately after he turned the merchants out of the temple, people who were lame and blind came to Jesus in the temple and he healed them—an act of direct contradiction to the temple laws which disallowed people with "defects" from being too close to the presence of God. Yet Jesus, the very incarnation of the Holy One, made a way for Gentiles and other excluded people to draw near.

Mark records that after the cleansing of the temple, the chief priests and teachers of the law "began looking for a way to kill him." In a real sense, Jesus sealed his fate with his angry insistence on the Gentiles' right to approach God.

- How have you felt excluded or unaccepted by people? By God? Describe that experience.

- What was the source of that feeling of being excluded from God's presence?

- Jesus healed the people who were lame and blind so that they could approach God as restored men and women. What does this tell you about the way God wants to move in your life? What might God want to restore in you?

- Jesus passionately paved the way for people to be with God. How can you do the same?

PRAYER

Start your prayer with this praise from the apostle John. Ask God to continue the work of healing in your life and help you pave the way for others to come into God's presence too.

"See what great love the Father has lavished on us, that we should be called children of God. And that is what we are!" (1 John 3:1).

GRACE ABUSE

Cheapening Grace and Robbing Its Power

You can know the law by heart without knowing the heart of it.

—PHILIP YANCEY [WSAAG, CHAPTER 15]

INTRODUCTION

The Pharisees who challenged Jesus with the case of the woman caught in adultery were strictly loyal to the law handed down from Moses—all 613 laws. But time and time again, Jesus pointed out that for all their careful adherence to the law, they missed the big picture. They were so caught up in legalism and the tempting idea that they could earn their way into God's good graces that they missed love for God and love for people.

At first glance legalism seems hard, but in fact freedom in Christ is harder. It is relatively easy not to murder, hard to reach out in love; easy to avoid a neighbor's bed, hard to keep a marriage alive; easy to pay taxes, hard to serve the poor. When living in freedom, I must remain open to the Spirit for guidance. I am more aware of what I have neglected than what I have achieved. I cannot hide behind a mask of behavior, like the hypocrites, nor can I hide behind facile comparisons with other Christians.

The Reformed theologian J. Gresham Machen wrote, "A low view of law leads to legalism in religion; a high view makes a seeker after grace."

The only way to avoid the hypocritical mask of legalism is through honesty that leads to repentance. As the Bible shows, God's grace can cover any sin, including murder, infidelity, or betrayal. Yet, by definition, grace must be received, and hypocrisy disguises our need to receive grace. When the masks fall, hypocrisy is exposed as an elaborate ruse to avoid grace.

WATCH VIDEO

Watch the video for session five. Add to the key points below notes of your own on anything that stands out or prompts a thought or a feeling.

The religious elite of Jesus's day focused so much on the small things that they forgot the big things—and were blinded to their own pride.

Instead of seeing good people and bad people, Jesus saw people in need of God's grace who knew it and people in need of God's grace who didn't realize it.

To receive grace, we must have open hands. We must admit our need.

The Sermon on the Mount both raises the moral ideals and lowers the safety net of grace.

We are called not to judge, but to show the world a better way, as Jesus did.

GROUP DISCUSSION

Choose the questions that work best for your group.

1. How are grace and Karma different?

2. C. S. Lewis said, "to condone an evil is simply to ignore it, to treat it as if it were good. But forgiveness needs to be accepted as well as offered if it is to be complete: and a man who admits no guilt can accept no forgiveness." What are the differences between condoning sin and forgiving sin?

3. **Read Matthew 5:3–6, 21–22.** How did Jesus, as Philip said, raise the moral ideals, and how did he lower the safety net of grace?

4. Bono said, "I'm holding out that Jesus took my sins onto the cross, because I know who I am, and I hope I don't have to depend on my own religiosity." How do we often rely on our own religiosity? What does relying on our own religiosity get us?

5. Some churches gradually lower the moral ideals to accommodate culture. Others raise the bar of grace so that people feel unwelcome. How have you seen this play out in your experience? Which way do you find yourself leaning toward more?

6. As Christians, how can we avoid being blinded by our own pride and the temptation to think we have it all together?

CLOSING PRAYER

*Spend a few minutes reflecting on today's discussion and then start
your prayer with these words:*

> *Jesus Christ, all these matters of giving grace and upholding
> moral standards, of forgiving rather than condoning sin, fade
> into the background when we remember the first and greatest
> commandment: to love you with all our hearts, minds, and
> souls. Give us wisdom to know how to do that in every situa-
> tion. Open our eyes to your extravagant love so that we might,
> in gratitude and humility, love others as you have loved us.*

SUGGESTED READING

For more thoughts and stories about grace from Philip Yancey,
read:

What's So Amazing About Grace?, chapters 13–16.

BETWEEN SESSIONS

These four individual studies take a closer look at biblical passages from the *What's So Amazing About Grace?* video and book and offer questions to prompt thoughts and ideas on how to apply the message of God's grace to your daily life.

PERSONAL JOURNEY 5.1

"Truly it is an evil to be full of faults; but it
is a still greater evil to be full of them and
to be unwilling to recognize them."
—Blaise Pascal [WSAAG, chapter 14]

Read John 8:2–11.

Philip writes, "The scene that John describes rattles me because by nature I identify more with the accusers than the accused. I deny far more than I confess. Cloaking my sins under a robe of respectability, I seldom if ever let myself get caught in a blatant, public indiscretion. Yet if I understand this story correctly, the sinful woman is the one nearest the kingdom of God. Indeed I can only advance in the kingdom if I become like that woman: trembling, humbled, without excuse, my palms open to receive God's grace."

With one sentence, Jesus brilliantly replaces two assumed categories, righteous and guilty, with two different categories: sinners who admit and sinners who deny. The woman caught in adultery helplessly admitted her guilt. But the Pharisees denied or repressed their own guilt. They needed open hands to receive the gift of grace. Dr. Paul Tournier describes it this way: "God blots out conscious guilt, but He brings to consciousness repressed guilt." [WSAAG, chapter 14]

- When you read the story of John 8, whom do you identify with the most? Why?

- James 4:6 says that God opposes the proud but shows favor to the humble. Why is humility so important to our ability to receive grace?

- How is confession a part of your relationship with God?

- What blind spot or repressed guilt might God be bringing to your consciousness?

PRAYER

Start your prayer with this passage from the Psalms and continue praying that God would humble your heart and reveal any blind spots in your life in need of grace.

"If you, LORD, kept a record of sins, Lord, who could stand? But with you there is forgiveness, so that we can, with reverence, serve you. I wait for the LORD, my whole being waits, and in his word I put my hope" (Psalm 130:3–5).

PERSONAL JOURNEY 5.2

*"Fear of man will prove to be a snare, but
whoever trusts in the LORD is kept safe."*
—PROVERBS 29:25

Read Acts 5:1–10.

The word *hypocrisy* means, simply, "putting on a mask."
Evidently Jesus himself coined the word, borrowing it from
the Greek actors who entertained crowds at an outdoor theater
near his home. It describes a person who puts on a face to make
a good impression.

This story is one of the most sobering passages in the New
Testament, and one of few that shows direct punishment.
Ananias and Sapphira had done a very good deed, selling
a piece of property and donating much of the proceeds to
the church. They did only one thing wrong: in an effort to
appear more spiritual, they acted as if they were donating *all*
the proceeds. In other words, they misrepresented themselves
spiritually. The harsh response to Ananias and Sapphira shows
how seriously God views hypocrisy. Expression of love for God
had, over time, evolved into ways of impressing others.

• How have you tried to appear more spiritual to others?

- What danger do masks pose to a relationship with God?

- What bothers, or challenges, you most about this story?

- How might we make sure that our expressions of love for God don't evolve into prideful ways of impressing others?

PRAYER

Start your prayer with this passage from the Psalms and continue praying, confessing any ways you've put on a spiritual mask.

"But who can discern their own errors? Forgive my hidden faults. Keep your servant also from willful sins; may they not rule over me. Then I will be blameless, innocent of great transgression. May these words of my mouth and this meditation of my heart be pleasing in your sight, LORD, my Rock, and my Redeemer" (Psalm 19:12–14).

PERSONAL JOURNEY 5.3

"Law merely indicated the sickness;
grace brought about the cure."
—PHILIP YANCEY [WSAAG, CHAPTER 15]

Read Romans 7:14–25, and John 15:9–11.

Legalism fails to do the one thing it is supposed to do: encourage obedience. In a strange twist, a system of strict laws actually puts new ideas of lawbreaking in a person's mind. Paul explains, "For I would not have known what coveting really was if the law had not said, 'Do not covet.' But sin, seizing the opportunity afforded by the commandment, produced in me every kind of covetous desire." In a demonstration of this principle, some surveys show that people raised in teetotaling denominations are three times as likely to become alcoholics.

When we make right behavior more important than a relationship with God, we direct all our energy to keeping or getting around "the law," rather than accomplishing the gospel. For believers who do not rebel, but rather strive sincerely to keep rules, legalism often leads to feelings of failure and lasting scars of shame—a strong contrast to the loving and joyful relationship with God that Jesus called us to in John 15.

- How have you experienced the reverse effect of the law that Paul describes, "But sin, seizing the opportunity afforded by the commandment, produced in me every kind of coveting" (Romans 7:8)?

- Paul still considered the law holy because it revealed what sin truly is and his need for God's grace (Romans 8:13). How has trying to keep the commandments brought you closer to God?

- How have you experienced the shame of legalism? How could you shift more from obedience fueled by avoiding failure with God to obedience fueled by love for God?

- What would you say to someone who wonders why they should try to live a good life, to obey God's commands, when God will give grace to them in the end anyway?

PRAYER

Start your prayer with this praise from the apostle Paul. Then continue your prayer by asking God to draw you deeper in loving relationship with him.

"Praise be to the God and Father of our Lord Jesus Christ, who has blessed us in the heavenly realms with every spiritual blessing in Christ. For he chose us in him before the creation of the world to be holy and blameless in his sight. In love he predestined us for adoption to sonship through Jesus Christ, in accordance with his pleasure and will—to the praise of his glorious grace, which he has freely given us in the One he loves" (Ephesians 1:3–6).

PERSONAL JOURNEY 5.4

"For the kingdom of God is not a matter of eating and drinking, but of righteousness, peace and joy in the Holy Spirit, because anyone who serves Christ in this way is pleasing to God and receives human approval."
—ROMANS 14:17–18

Read Matthew 23:23–24 and Romans 14:1–12.

It is doubtful that Jesus really cared what the Pharisees ate or how many times they washed their hands. But he did care that they imposed extremism on others and that they focused on trivialities, neglecting more weighty matters. The same teachers who tithed their kitchen spices had little to say about the injustice and oppression in Palestine. And when

Jesus healed a person on the Sabbath, his critics seemed far more concerned about protocol than about the sick person.

The modern-day church has had its own bouts with legalistic trivialities, having much to say about tattoos and piercings and certain genres of music while saying very little about racial injustice and world hunger.

The low point of legalism played itself out at Jesus's execution: the Pharisees took pains to avoid entering Pilate's palace before the Passover feast and arranged the crucifixion so as not to interfere with Sabbath rules. Thus, the greatest crime in history was carried out with strict attention to legalistic detail. [chapter 15]

- Christians can be defensive and judgmental when it comes to the ways they observe their faith. What do you think is at the heart of this passionate response?

- What trivialities do our modern Christian communities obsess over?

- How have you seen protocol or trivialities get in the way of Christians showing justice, mercy, and faithfulness?

- There is much division in our world today, and in the church. How might we live as fully convinced in our own minds about how we practice our faith while still respecting others whose faith in Jesus Christ has led them to different decisions? (See Romans 14:5.)

PRAYER

Start your prayer with these words inspired by Colossians 3:12–15. Then continue your prayer by asking God to reveal to you any areas where trivialities have become more important than justice, mercy, and faithfulness.

As God's people, holy and dearly loved, help us to clothe ourselves with compassion, kindness, humility, gentleness, and patience, bearing with each other and forgiving one another as you do for us. And over all virtues, let us put on love and peace, which bind us together in perfect unity.

DISPENSING GRACE

How Can We Do It?

Of one hundred men, one will read the Bible; the ninety-nine will read the Christian.

—DWIGHT L. MOODY [WSAAG, CHAPTER 19]

INTRODUCTION

A renewal of spirituality in the United States will not descend from the top down; if it occurs at all, it will start at the grass roots and grow from the bottom up.

Jesus's images portray the kingdom of God as a kind of secret force. Sheep among wolves, treasure hidden in a field, the tiniest seed in the garden, a pinch of yeast worked into bread dough, a sprinkling of salt on meat—all these hint at a movement that works within society, changing it from the inside out.

What if Christians used that same approach in a secular society and succeeded? "In a world the Christians are a colony of the true home," said Dietrich Bonhoeffer. But all too often the church holds up a mirror reflecting back the society around it, rather than a window revealing a different way.

Perhaps Christians should work harder toward cultivating little establishments of the kingdom that point to our true home. If the world despises a notorious sinner, the church will instead love her. If the world cuts off aid to the poor and the suffering, the church will offer food and healing. That at least is the vision of the church in the New Testament: a colony of heaven in a hostile word.

The world thirsts for grace. And when grace descends, the world falls silent before it.

WATCH VIDEO

Watch the video for session six. Add to the key points below notes of your own on anything that stands out or prompts a thought or a feeling.

The gospel is good news that we are called to share—especially with people who may be skeptical and hostile.

Three groups of people who are especially effective at dispensing grace: Activists, Artists, and Pilgrims.

Like salt and yeast, simple acts of grace affect our entire society.

Our main distinction as Christians is that we've admitted our need for God's grace—we've held out open hands. All the good in us comes as a gift from God that we should then want to introduce to others.

The way of grace is not easy. But if we make dispensing grace a priority, then the world would understand the gospel as truly good news.

GROUP DISCUSSION

Choose the questions that work best for your group.

1. How would you answer the question Philip poses in the beginning of the video: How can we best spread the good news of the gospel, especially to people who may be skeptical and hostile?

2. Where do you see yourself among the three groups effective at dispensing grace—Activists, Artists, and Pilgrims? How might you be uniquely positioned to dispense grace in your social circles?

3. Why do Christians often come across as "holier than thou"? When have you found yourself fighting the sense of feeling superior to others?

4. What would a subversive, radically gracious church look like in the modern United States?

5. What do you foresee as frustrations and challenges to being a dispenser of grace, bit by bit, conversation to conversation, person to person?

6. **Read Romans 12:9–21.** What stands out to you most? What is one way you can align your life more with this gracious way of living?

CLOSING PRAYER

*Spend a few minutes reflecting on today's discussion and then start
your prayer with these words:*

> *Lord, you have given us such profound grace and we humbly
> acknowledge our desperate need for it. Thank you for your
> love and forgiveness which draw us again and again back
> into your presence. And now as we go about our days, please
> give us willing hearts and hands to give grace wherever we go.*

SUGGESTED READING

For more thoughts and stories about grace from Philip Yancey,
read:

What's So Amazing About Grace?, chapters 17–20.

FINAL STUDIES

These four individual studies take a closer look at biblical passages from the *What's So Amazing About Grace?* video and book and offer questions to prompt thoughts and ideas on how to apply the message of God's grace to your daily life.

PERSONAL JOURNEY 6.1

"I see the confusion of politics and religion as
one of the greatest barriers to grace."
—PHILIP YANCEY [WSAAG, CHAPTER 17]

Read Mark 12:13–17.

The Pharisees and Herodians wanted to trap Jesus: did he favor God or government? But looking at the life of Jesus, we find that he did not let any institution interfere with his love for individuals. Jewish policies forbade him to speak with a Samaritan woman, let alone one with a checkered background, but Jesus spoke with her at length. His disciples included Matthew, a tax collector who was viewed as a traitor by his people, and the Zealot Simon, a member of the superpatriot party. He praised the countercultural John the Baptist.

He met with Nicodemus, an observant Pharisee, and also with a Roman centurion.

The church is becoming more and more politicized, and an unraveling society takes note when we emphasize mercy less and morality more. Politics draws lines between people, but Jesus's love cuts across those lines and dispenses grace. That does not mean, of course, that Christians should not involve themselves in politics. It simply means that as we do so we must not let the rules of power displace the command to love.

- As citizens of heaven, what role should we play in politics?

- As Christians, how do we keep our focus on the kingdom of God while still trying to manage our vote and political influence?

- How does being a grace dispenser change the way you engage with political issues? How does it change the way you relate to those across political party lines?

- What should our response be when our morals are at odds with the government? (See Titus 3:1–2; Romans 13:1–7.)

PRAYER

Say these verses as a prayer. Then continue praying by asking God to give you wisdom for engaging in social and political arenas.

"All the nations you have made will come and worship before you, Lord; they will bring glory to your name. For you are great and do marvelous deeds; you alone are God. Teach me your way, LORD, that I may rely on your faithfulness; give me an undivided heart, that I may fear your name. I will praise you, Lord my God, with all my heart; I will glorify your name forever. For great is your love toward me" (Psalm 86:9–13).

PERSONAL JOURNEY 6.2

"For all those who exalt themselves will be humbled, and those who humble themselves will be exalted."

—LUKE 14:11

Read Luke 19:1–10.

Readers of the Gospels marvel at Jesus's ability to move with ease among the sinners and outcasts. The sinners were honest about themselves and had no pretense. The purported saints, in contrast, put on airs, judged him, and sought to catch him in a moral trap. In the end it was the saints, not the sinners, who arrested Jesus.

As a Jewish tax collector employed by the Romans, Zacchaeus was considered a traitor to his own people. Yet Jesus not only spoke kindly to him but went to his house. The people were repulsed: He has gone to be the guest of a sinner.

Like the crowd, we sometimes cling to a false sense of moral superiority, thinking to ourselves that we're not really all that bad. Yet it was Zacchaeus, the sinner, who quickly repented and made restitution, and his house was flooded with the grace of salvation. The only prerequisite was a humble and responsive heart—no mask, no pretense.

- Did Zacchaeus repent or did Jesus show grace first?

- In what ways might you hold onto masks or pretense in your prayers and relationship with God? With your friends and family? With yourself?

- How does a false sense of superiority keep us distanced from one another?

- Zacchaeus likely understood the principles of repentance and honesty more than the religious elite. He put those principles into action. What does this mean for Christians today?

PRAYER

Pray this Psalm and continue your prayer as honestly as possible about all that is on your heart and mind.

"My heart is not proud, LORD, my eyes are not haughty; I do not concern myself with great matters or things too wonderful for me. But I have calmed and quieted myself, I am like a weaned child with its mother; like a weaned child I am content. Israel, put your hope in the LORD both now and forevermore" (Psalm 131).

PERSONAL JOURNEY 6.3

"But whoever drinks the water I give them will never thirst. Indeed, the water I give them will become in them a spring of water welling up to eternal life."

—JOHN 4:14

Read John 4:7–26.

Grace changes the way we see people—inside the church and outside. It teaches us that every human soul is a sinner loved by God. Some of us have strayed very far from home, but even so the Father stands ready to welcome us back with joy.

John gives an account of how Jesus related to people who didn't practice the same morals as he did. In those days, the husband initiated divorce: this Samaritan woman had been dumped by five different men. Jesus could have begun by pointing out what a mess the woman had made of her life. Yet he did not dwell on her moral flaws. Rather he said, in effect, *I sense that you are very thirsty.* Jesus went on to tell her that the water she was drinking would never satisfy and then offered her living water to quench her thirst forever.

After visiting various ministries to AIDS victims, priest Henri Nouwen was deeply moved by their sad stories and commented, "They want love so bad, it's literally killing them." He saw them as thirsty people panting after the wrong kind of water.

• When have you been thirsty for the wrong kind of water?

- How would you describe the default lens with which you view people you don't know? What things do you notice about them, what thoughts come to mind?

- Jesus's relatively brief conversation with the Samaritan woman led to the entire village hearing the gospel (John 4:39). What small act can you do today to bring a bit of grace into a relationship with someone you don't agree with?

- When you encounter someone of whom you morally disapprove, what can you do to remind yourself to view them, through the lens of grace, as thirsty people?

PRAYER

Start your prayer with this passage inspired by Ephesians 4:31–5:2. Listen for how God might be prompting you to act.

Lord, help me to get rid of all bitterness, anger, pride, and judgment. Help me to be kind and compassionate to others, forgiving others, just as you have forgiven me. Guide me, as your dearly loved child, to walk in the way of love, just as Christ loved me and gave himself up for me.

PERSONAL JOURNEY 6.4

"The kingdom of God thrives where its subjects follow the desires of the King."

—PHILIP YANCEY [WSAAG, CHAPTER 19]

Read Matthew 13:31–33.

Jesus described his kingdom as a small seed that grows into a great tree, and a pinch of yeast that causes a whole batch of dough to rise. He compared the work of Christians to salt's role in preserving meat (Matthew 5:13). You do not need a shovelful of salt to preserve a slab of ham; a dusting will suffice.

Jesus did not leave an organized host of followers, for he knew that a handful of salt would gradually work its way through the mightiest empire in the world. Against all odds, the great institutions of Rome gradually crumbled, but the little band to whom Jesus gave these images prevailed and continues on today. Christians behave somewhat like spies, living in one world while our deepest allegiance belongs to another.

It would seem that such a way of living would be simplified in a nation seemingly founded on Christian principles. In fact, some observers have called the United States the most religious nation on earth. If true, that fact leads to a bracing question, as articulated by Dallas Willard: Shouldn't a quarter pound of salt be having more effect on a pound of meat?

- In your opinion, what are some of the reasons why Christians aren't as effective in the United States?

- What are the challenges or obstacles that keep you from being as effective at giving grace as you'd like?

- Matthew 5:13 says that when salt loses its saltiness, it is no longer good for anything. What practices can you do to keep your "saltiness" and remain grounded in grace?

- The seed, yeast, and salt—these take time to do their transformative work. How can we make sure we do not give up being grace dispensers when there seems to be little or no effect?

PRAYER

Say these verses as a prayer and then continue your prayer by asking God to show you what opportunities there are in your life to spread grace like salt.

"Let us not become weary in doing good, for at the proper time we will reap a harvest if we do not give up. Therefore, as we have opportunity, let us do good to all people" (Galatians 6:9–10).